Forging Peace: The 2000-2002 British Military Intervention in Sierra Leone

Copyright Page

TITLE: Forging Peace: The 2000-2002 British Military Intervention in Sierra Leone

1ST Edition

Table of Contents

Forging Peace: The 2000-2002 British Military Intervention in Sierra Leone

By Roberto Miguel Rodriguez

Introduction:

- Brief overview of the 2000-2002 British Military Intervention in Sierra Leone

- Importance of studying this intervention for historians and its relevance to understanding conflict resolution and peacekeeping efforts

Historical Context

- Examination of Sierra Leone's civil war, causes, and key actors

- Overview of previous international intervention attempts and their limitations

- Analysis of the factors leading to the British intervention

Motives behind the British Intervention

- Exploration of the political and strategic motives that influenced the decision to intervene

- Examination of the UK's interests in the region and its historical relationship with Sierra Leone

- Discussion of the humanitarian aspect as a driving force behind the intervention

Role of the British Army

- Analysis of the British Army's involvement in Sierra Leone's civil war

- Evaluation of their military tactics and strategies in ending the conflict

- Examination of the challenges faced by the British forces and their response

Impact on Post-war Reconstruction

- Assessment of the immediate impact of the intervention on Sierra Leone's post-war reconstruction efforts

- Analysis of the role played by the British in stabilizing the country and restoring governance

- Evaluation of the long-term socio-economic impacts of the intervention on Sierra Leone's development

International Community's Response

- Examination of the international community's response to the British intervention

- Assessment of the effectiveness of international support in aiding the intervention efforts

- Analysis of the lessons learned for future peacekeeping missions

Local Militias and Rebel Groups

- Examination of the role played by local militias and rebel groups during the intervention

- Evaluation of their interactions with the British forces and their impact on the conflict resolution process

UK-Sierra Leone Government Relationship

- Analysis of the UK's relationship with the Sierra Leone government before, during, and after the military intervention

- Evaluation of the dynamics between the two parties and the implications for the intervention's success

Comparison with other Peacekeeping Missions

- Comparative analysis of the British intervention in Sierra Leone with other international peacekeeping missions

- Evaluation of the similarities, differences, and lessons learned from these missions

Conclusion:

- Summary of the key findings and insights gained from studying the 2000-2002 British Military Intervention in Sierra Leone

- Importance of understanding this intervention for future conflict resolution efforts

- Final thoughts on the long-term impact of the intervention on Sierra Leone's development and stability.

Chapter 1: The 2000-2002 British Military Intervention to End Sierra Leone's Civil War

Background and Context of Sierra Leone's Civil War

Sierra Leone's Civil War, which spanned from 1991 to 2002, was a devastating conflict that resulted in the loss of thousands of lives and the displacement of countless more. In order to fully understand the events that unfolded during this period, it is important to examine the background and context that led to the outbreak of the war.

Sierra Leone gained its independence from Britain in 1961, but the legacy of colonialism left the country grappling with political instability and social unrest. The government struggled to address the economic disparities and ethnic tensions that plagued the nation, leading to widespread frustration and discontent among the population.

The civil war was ignited by the Revolutionary United Front (RUF), a rebel group led by Foday Sankoh. The RUF sought to overthrow the government and gain control of Sierra Leone's rich diamond mines. Their campaign of violence and brutality, characterized by mutilations, amputations, and the recruitment of child soldiers, quickly gained international attention.

In response to the escalating violence and the deteriorating humanitarian situation, the international community, led by the United Kingdom, intervened militarily in Sierra Leone in 2000. The British military intervention aimed to restore peace and stability to the country, protect civilians, and disarm the rebel groups.

The role of the British Army in Sierra Leone's Civil War was multifaceted. British forces worked alongside the Sierra Leonean army to combat the rebel groups, providing training, equipment, and logistical support. They also played a crucial role in the demobilization and reintegration of former combatants, as well as the establishment of a new democratic government.

The impact of the British military intervention on Sierra Leone's post-war reconstruction was significant. The intervention helped pave the way for the country's recovery and laid the foundation for long-term development. The British Army's tactics and strategies, such as community engagement and the establishment of security zones, were effective in ending the civil war and restoring a sense of security.

Furthermore, the humanitarian aspect of the British military intervention cannot be overlooked. British forces provided vital humanitarian assistance, including medical care, food aid, and support for displaced populations. This assistance was crucial in alleviating the suffering of Sierra Leone's population and facilitating the country's recovery.

The international community's response to the British intervention in Sierra Leone was generally positive. The intervention was seen as a model for future peacekeeping missions, highlighting the importance of a comprehensive approach that combines military action with humanitarian assistance and long-term development efforts.

Examining the role of local militias and rebel groups during the British intervention in Sierra Leone is crucial to understanding the complexities of the conflict. These groups, including the RUF, posed significant challenges to the British forces and were responsible for widespread human rights abuses.

The relationship between the UK and the Sierra Leone government before, during, and after the military intervention was complex. While the intervention was welcomed by the government as a means of restoring peace and stability, there were tensions and disagreements over issues such as governance and resource allocation.

Comparing the British intervention in Sierra Leone with other international peacekeeping missions provides valuable insights into the effectiveness of different approaches and strategies. The lessons learned from Sierra Leone have informed subsequent interventions and shaped the evolution of peacekeeping practices.

Finally, assessing the long-term socio-economic impacts of the British military intervention on Sierra Leone's development is essential. The intervention played a crucial role in jumpstarting the country's recovery and laying the groundwork for sustainable development. However, challenges remain, including addressing the root causes of the conflict, promoting economic growth, and ensuring social justice.

In conclusion, understanding the background and context of Sierra Leone's Civil War is essential to comprehending the complexities of the conflict and the subsequent British military intervention. This subchapter provides a comprehensive overview of the historical, political, and strategic factors that shaped the war and its aftermath, addressing the interests of historians and the various niches interested in this topic.

Causes and Escalation of the Civil War

The civil war in Sierra Leone, which lasted from 1991 to 2002, was a complex conflict that had deep-rooted causes and escalated due to various factors. Understanding these causes and the subsequent escalation is crucial to comprehending the context in which the British military intervention took place.

The civil war in Sierra Leone can be traced back to several interrelated causes. One of the primary factors was the marginalization and exclusion of certain ethnic and regional groups from political power by successive governments. The lack of inclusive governance created a breeding ground for resentment and grievances, which ultimately fueled the conflict.

Another significant cause of the civil war was the economic inequality and the exploitation of natural resources. Sierra Leone's vast mineral wealth, particularly its diamond reserves, became a source of contention and a driver of conflict. Rebel groups, such as the Revolutionary United Front (RUF), emerged to exploit these resources and finance their insurgency, further exacerbating the conflict.

The escalation of the civil war can be attributed to a range of factors. The RUF's brutal tactics, including the use of child soldiers and systematic human rights abuses, contributed to the worsening violence and instability. The group's strategy of terrorizing civilians and committing atrocities created a climate of fear and further destabilized the country.

Additionally, the involvement of external actors, such as neighboring countries and international arms dealers, played a significant role in escalating the conflict. These actors provided support to rebel groups, prolonging the war and making it increasingly difficult to find a peaceful resolution.

The civil war in Sierra Leone reached a critical point in the late 1990s when rebel forces launched a series of attacks on the capital, Freetown. The intensification of violence and the threat posed to the civilian population prompted the international community to intervene, leading to the British military intervention in 2000.

In conclusion, the causes of the civil war in Sierra Leone were multi-faceted, including political marginalization, economic inequality, and resource exploitation. The escalated violence and instability were driven by the ruthless tactics of rebel groups, the involvement of external actors, and the threat posed to the capital. These factors set the stage for the British military intervention, which aimed to bring an end to the conflict and restore peace in Sierra Leone. Understanding the causes and escalation of the civil war is crucial for historians studying the impact of the British intervention, the role of the British Army, the effectiveness of military tactics, and the long-term socio-economic impacts on Sierra Leone's development.

International Response to Sierra Leone's Civil War

The civil war in Sierra Leone, which ravaged the nation from 1991 to 2002, drew significant attention and intervention from the international community. This subchapter explores the various responses and actions taken by the international community during this period, shedding light on their effectiveness and impact on Sierra Leone's post-war reconstruction.

The 2000-2002 British Military Intervention in Sierra Leone played a pivotal role in ending the civil war and restoring stability to the country. Historians have extensively studied the motives behind the British intervention, analyzing the political and strategic factors that shaped this decision. By examining these motives, historians can gain a deeper understanding of the UK's relationship with the Sierra Leone government before, during, and after the military intervention.

The effectiveness of British military tactics and strategies in ending Sierra Leone's civil war is another crucial aspect to explore. By assessing the effectiveness of these tactics, historians can evaluate the role played by the British army in bringing peace to the war-torn nation. The comparison of the British intervention in Sierra Leone with other international peacekeeping missions can provide valuable insights into the unique challenges and successes of the British approach.

While the military intervention was primarily aimed at restoring peace, the humanitarian aspect of the British intervention cannot be overlooked. The international community responded to the crisis by providing humanitarian aid and support to the affected population. Examining the humanitarian efforts and their impact on the ground can provide a comprehensive understanding of the overall response to the crisis.

Furthermore, it is essential to analyze the role of local militias and rebel groups during the British intervention. This examination will shed light on the complexities of the conflict and the challenges faced by the international forces in navigating the intricate web of local dynamics.

Finally, the long-term socio-economic impacts of the British military intervention on Sierra Leone's development are of utmost importance. Historians can assess the changes brought about by the intervention, both positive and negative, and provide insights into the challenges that the nation faced in its post-war reconstruction.

By delving into these various aspects of the international response to Sierra Leone's civil war, historians can gain a comprehensive understanding of the multifaceted nature of the conflict and its aftermath. This subchapter aims to provide a detailed analysis of the international community's involvement and its impact on Sierra Leone's journey towards peace and development.

Chapter 2: Role of the British Army in Sierra Leone's Civil War

Deployment of British Troops to Sierra Leone

The deployment of British troops to Sierra Leone in the early 2000s marked a significant turning point in the country's history, as well as a pivotal moment in international peacekeeping efforts. This subchapter explores the various aspects of the British military intervention in Sierra Leone, analyzing its political and strategic motives, the effectiveness of its tactics and strategies, and its impact on the country's post-war reconstruction.

The decision to deploy British troops to Sierra Leone was driven by multiple factors. One of the primary motives was the need to end the brutal civil war that had plagued the country for over a decade. The British government recognized the importance of restoring peace and stability to Sierra Leone, not only for humanitarian reasons but also to prevent the conflict from spilling over into neighboring countries. Additionally, the intervention aimed to protect British interests in the region, as Sierra Leone was a former colony and held valuable mineral resources.

The British Army played a crucial role in Sierra Leone's civil war, working alongside the Sierra Leonean government forces to defeat rebel groups such as the Revolutionary United Front. The effectiveness of British military tactics and strategies was evident in their successful efforts to disarm and demobilize combatants, establish security, and restore law and order. Their approach emphasized a combination of military force, diplomacy, and development assistance, which proved instrumental in ending the conflict.

The humanitarian aspect of the British military intervention cannot be overstated. British troops not only protected civilians from violence but also provided much-needed aid, including medical assistance, food, and shelter. Their presence instilled a sense of security and hope among the population, enabling them to rebuild their lives and communities in the aftermath of the war.

The international community responded positively to the British intervention in Sierra Leone, recognizing its significance in ending the conflict and restoring peace. The United Nations, in particular, played a key role in supporting and coordinating the intervention, showcasing the effectiveness of international cooperation in addressing complex conflicts.

Examining the role of local militias and rebel groups during the British intervention provides valuable insights into the dynamics of the conflict. It highlights the challenges faced by British troops in dealing with non-state actors and the importance of engaging with and disarming these groups to achieve long-term peace.

The relationship between the UK and the Sierra Leonean government before, during, and after the military intervention is a crucial aspect to explore. It sheds light on the dynamics of international intervention and the complexities of post-conflict governance.

Comparing the British intervention in Sierra Leone with other international peacekeeping missions allows for a broader understanding of the challenges and successes in such operations. It provides valuable lessons for future interventions and contributes to the ongoing discourse on peacekeeping strategies.

Finally, evaluating the long-term socio-economic impacts of the British military intervention on Sierra Leone's development is essential. It examines the extent to which the intervention contributed to sustainable peace, economic growth, and social progress in the country.

In conclusion, the deployment of British troops to Sierra Leone had far-reaching implications for both the country and international peacekeeping efforts. Analyzing the political and strategic motives, the effectiveness of military tactics, and the impact on post-war reconstruction provides valuable insights for historians and those interested in the complexities of conflict resolution and sustainable development.

Objectives and Mandate of the British Military Intervention

The British Military Intervention in Sierra Leone, which took place from 2000 to 2002, had a clear set of objectives and a well-defined mandate. This subchapter aims to provide historians and those interested in the specific niches surrounding the intervention with an in-depth understanding of its goals and purpose.

At the heart of the British intervention was the objective to end Sierra Leone's devastating civil war, which had been raging since 1991. The conflict had caused immense suffering and humanitarian crisis, prompting the international community to take action. The British military, with its expertise in peacekeeping operations, was tasked with bringing stability and security to the war-torn nation.

The mandate of the intervention encompassed several key aspects. First and foremost, it sought to disarm and demobilize the rebel groups that had been terrorizing the population for years. This involved a comprehensive strategy to seize weapons, dismantle rebel camps, and reintegrate former combatants into society.

Additionally, the British military intervention aimed to support the Sierra Leonean government in reestablishing its authority and governance structures. This included training and mentoring the national army and police forces, as well as assisting in the restoration of basic public services such as healthcare and education.

Another crucial aspect of the intervention was to provide humanitarian assistance to the affected population. British forces played a vital role in delivering aid, providing medical assistance, and facilitating the return of displaced persons to their homes.

Furthermore, the intervention aimed to create a conducive environment for post-war reconstruction and development. This involved promoting political dialogue, supporting the establishment of a Truth and Reconciliation Commission, and facilitating the reintegration of former combatants into civilian life.

The objectives and mandate of the British military intervention in Sierra Leone were driven by a combination of political and strategic motives. On one hand, the intervention aimed to protect British interests in the region, including safeguarding the country's diamond trade and preventing the conflict from spilling over into neighboring countries. On the other hand, it was driven by a genuine commitment to peace, stability, and the protection of human rights.

Overall, the British Military Intervention in Sierra Leone played a crucial role in ending the civil war and laying the foundations for post-war reconstruction. Its objectives and mandate were multifaceted, addressing not only military aspects but also humanitarian and development needs. The intervention's effectiveness in achieving its goals, as well as its long-term impacts on Sierra Leone's development, will be examined in subsequent chapters.

Collaboration with Sierra Leone's National Army and Security Forces

The collaboration between the British military and Sierra Leone's National Army and Security Forces played a crucial role in the success of the 2000-2002 British military intervention in Sierra Leone. This subchapter will explore the dynamics of this collaboration, its challenges, and its impact on the overall outcome of the intervention.

From the outset, it was clear that a strong partnership with Sierra Leone's National Army and Security Forces was essential for the success of the intervention. The British military recognized the importance of working hand in hand with local forces to restore stability and security in the country. By collaborating with the national army, the British aimed to build the capacity of the local forces, enhance their professionalism, and establish a sustainable security apparatus.

However, the collaboration was not without its challenges. The Sierra Leonean forces were severely weakened and demoralized due to years of civil war. They lacked the necessary resources, training, and equipment to effectively carry out their duties. The British military had to overcome these obstacles and provide the necessary support, including training, mentorship, and logistical assistance.

The collaboration between the British military and the Sierra Leonean forces yielded significant results. The joint operations conducted by both forces helped to weaken rebel groups and restore law and order in the country. The British military's expertise in counter-insurgency tactics and strategies proved invaluable in training and guiding the Sierra Leonean forces.

Moreover, the collaboration had a long-term impact on Sierra Leone's post-war reconstruction. By building the capacity of the national army and security forces, the intervention laid the foundation for a more stable and secure future. The improved security situation allowed for the implementation of development programs, the return of displaced populations, and the rebuilding of infrastructure.

In conclusion, the collaboration between the British military and Sierra Leone's National Army and Security Forces played a crucial role in the success of the 2000-2002 British military intervention in Sierra Leone. Despite the challenges, the partnership led to significant improvements in the security situation and laid the groundwork for long-term stability and development. This chapter will provide a detailed analysis of the collaboration, its impact, and its lessons for future peacekeeping missions.

Chapter 3: Impact of the British Military Intervention on Sierra Leone's Post-War Reconstruction

Restoration of Security and Disarmament of Rebel Groups

The restoration of security and disarmament of rebel groups was a crucial aspect of the 2000-2002 British military intervention in Sierra Leone. This subchapter aims to delve into the strategies employed by the British Army to achieve this objective, as well as the impact these efforts had on Sierra Leone's post-war reconstruction.

The British intervention in Sierra Leone was prompted by the urgent need to end the country's devastating civil war, which had been fueled by rebel groups such as the Revolutionary United Front (RUF) and the Armed Forces Revolutionary Council (AFRC). These groups had terrorized the civilian population, committing heinous acts of violence and recruiting child soldiers.

To restore security, the British Army undertook a multifaceted approach. Firstly, they deployed a significant number of troops to provide a robust and visible presence across the country. This not only reassured the population but also deterred rebel groups from continuing their activities. The British soldiers conducted regular patrols and established control over key areas, gradually eroding the rebels' influence.

Disarmament was another critical component of the intervention. The British Army implemented a disarmament campaign aimed at persuading rebel fighters to surrender their weapons voluntarily. This process involved setting up disarmament centers and providing incentives for rebels to lay down their arms. The success of this campaign was evident in the large number of weapons collected, which significantly weakened the rebel groups' military capabilities.

The restoration of security and disarmament of rebel groups had a profound impact on Sierra Leone's post-war reconstruction. By eliminating the immediate threat posed by rebel forces, the intervention created a conducive environment for stability and development. It allowed the Sierra Leone government, with the support of the international community, to focus on rebuilding the country's institutions, infrastructure, and economy.

Moreover, the disarmament process facilitated the reintegration of former combatants into society. The British intervention prioritized the demobilization and rehabilitation of ex-combatants, providing them with training, education, and assistance in finding employment. This not only contributed to the individuals' reintegration but also reduced the likelihood of them being re-recruited by rebel groups or turning to criminal activities.

In conclusion, the restoration of security and disarmament of rebel groups was a pivotal aspect of the 2000-2002 British military intervention in Sierra Leone. By deploying troops and implementing a comprehensive disarmament campaign, the British Army successfully eliminated the immediate threat posed by rebel forces. This allowed for the subsequent reconstruction efforts and facilitated the reintegration of former combatants. The impact of these efforts on Sierra Leone's development was significant, laying the foundation for long-term stability and socio-economic growth.

Assistance in Rebuilding Sierra Leone's Institutions and Infrastructure

The 2000-2002 British Military Intervention in Sierra Leone was not only focused on ending the civil war but also on rebuilding the nation's institutions and infrastructure. This subchapter delves into the crucial role played by the British military in assisting Sierra Leone in its post-war reconstruction efforts.

After the civil war, Sierra Leone was left in a state of disarray, with its institutions and infrastructure severely damaged. Recognizing the importance of establishing a stable and functioning society, the British military took on the task of assisting in the rebuilding process.

One of the key areas of focus was the restoration of Sierra Leone's institutions, including the judiciary, police force, and civil administration. The British military provided training and support to local personnel, helping to strengthen these institutions and ensure their effectiveness. This assistance was vital in restoring the rule of law and promoting good governance in Sierra Leone.

Infrastructure development was another critical aspect of the reconstruction efforts. The British military worked closely with local authorities to rebuild roads, bridges, schools, and hospitals that had been destroyed during the war. This infrastructure development not only improved the quality of life for the people of Sierra Leone but also laid the foundation for long-term economic growth.

The assistance provided by the British military went beyond physical reconstruction. They also played a significant role in providing humanitarian aid to the war-affected population. This included the distribution of food, water, and medical supplies, as well as the establishment of refugee camps and safe zones.

The international community played a crucial role in supporting Sierra Leone's post-war reconstruction, and the British military intervention was a key part of this effort. Their strategic motives were driven by a desire to bring stability to the region and prevent the spread of conflict. The effectiveness of their tactics and strategies in ending the civil war and facilitating reconstruction cannot be understated.

In conclusion, the British military intervention in Sierra Leone not only brought an end to the civil war but also provided much-needed assistance in rebuilding the nation's institutions and infrastructure. Their efforts in restoring Sierra Leone's institutions, promoting good governance, and facilitating infrastructure development were essential in laying the groundwork for long-term socio-economic development. The impact of their assistance continues to be felt in Sierra Leone to this day, making the British military intervention a significant chapter in the history of international peacekeeping missions.

Socio-Economic Initiatives and Development Projects

The 2000-2002 British Military Intervention in Sierra Leone was not only aimed at ending the civil war but also focused on long-term socio-economic initiatives and development projects. These initiatives played a crucial role in the post-war reconstruction of Sierra Leone, bringing about significant changes in various sectors of the country.

One of the key initiatives undertaken by the British military was the establishment of infrastructure projects. The army worked diligently to repair and rebuild roads, bridges, and other vital transportation networks that had been severely damaged during the war. This not only facilitated movement and trade within the country but also helped in linking remote areas with major towns and cities, thereby promoting economic growth and development.

Another important aspect of the socio-economic initiatives was the emphasis on education and healthcare. British forces worked closely with local authorities to refurbish schools and hospitals, ensuring that children had access to quality education and that healthcare facilities were readily available to the population. The intervention also focused on training local teachers and healthcare professionals, empowering them to take charge of these sectors in the long run.

Furthermore, the British intervention aimed to revive the agricultural sector, which was the backbone of Sierra Leone's economy. The military collaborated with local farmers, providing them with improved seed varieties, modern farming techniques, and tools. This not only boosted agricultural productivity but also helped in stabilizing food security in the country.

In addition to these initiatives, the British military intervention supported small-scale enterprises and entrepreneurship. Microcredit programs were established to provide financial assistance to individuals interested in starting their own businesses. This created employment opportunities and stimulated economic growth at the grassroots level.

Overall, the socio-economic initiatives and development projects implemented during the British military intervention in Sierra Leone had a profound impact on the country's post-war reconstruction and long-term development. These initiatives helped in rebuilding infrastructure, revitalizing education and healthcare systems, promoting agriculture, and fostering economic growth. The British intervention not only brought an end to the civil war but also laid the foundation for a more prosperous and stable Sierra Leone.

Chapter 4: Analysis of the Political and Strategic Motives behind the British Intervention in Sierra Leone

British Interests and Foreign Policy Considerations

The 2000-2002 British Military Intervention in Sierra Leone was driven by a range of British interests and foreign policy considerations. This subchapter aims to provide a comprehensive analysis of these factors and their impact on the intervention.

From a historical perspective, understanding the motives behind the British intervention is crucial. Historians examining this period can delve into the role of the British Army in Sierra Leone's Civil War, assessing its effectiveness in ending the conflict. The military tactics and strategies employed by the British forces can be evaluated, shedding light on their success in bringing peace to the war-torn nation.

Foreign policy considerations played a significant role in shaping the British intervention. Historians can explore the political and strategic motives that drove this decision, analyzing the UK's relationship with the Sierra Leone government before, during, and after the intervention. This examination can provide insights into the international community's response to the British intervention and compare it with other peacekeeping missions, highlighting the unique aspects of this particular intervention.

Furthermore, historians can explore the humanitarian aspect of the British military intervention in Sierra Leone. The impact on Sierra Leone's post-war reconstruction can be assessed, focusing on its long-term socio-economic impacts and development. Attention can also be given to the role of local militias and rebel groups during the intervention, examining their influence and interactions with the British forces.

Throughout this subchapter, historians can gain a comprehensive understanding of the British interests and foreign policy considerations that shaped the 2000-2002 intervention in Sierra Leone. By analyzing the historical context, political motivations, and the effectiveness of military tactics, a clearer picture emerges of the UK's role in ending the civil war and its impact on Sierra Leone's reconstruction. This analysis contributes to a deeper understanding of international peacekeeping efforts, the complexities of post-conflict development, and the dynamics of the UK's relationship with Sierra Leone.

Regional and Global Implications of the Sierra Leone Conflict

The Sierra Leone conflict, which persisted for over a decade, had significant regional and global implications that shaped the course of history and influenced various stakeholders. This subchapter will delve into the far-reaching consequences of the conflict, examining the impact on neighboring countries, the international community, and the long-term socio-economic development of Sierra Leone.

The civil war in Sierra Leone had profound ramifications for neighboring countries in West Africa. The conflict spilled across borders, leading to the destabilization of the entire region. Rebel groups, such as the Revolutionary United Front (RUF), exploited weak governance structures and porous borders to seek refuge in neighboring countries, exacerbating the already fragile security situation. This resulted in the displacement of thousands of people and the proliferation of arms and mercenaries throughout the region. The subchapter will provide a comprehensive analysis of the regional implications, focusing on the role of neighboring countries in supporting or combating the conflict.

Furthermore, the Sierra Leone conflict attracted international attention, prompting various actors to respond to the crisis. The British military intervention from 2000 to 2002 played a pivotal role in ending the civil war and restoring stability. This subchapter will critically assess the political and strategic motives behind the British intervention, exploring the effectiveness of their tactics and strategies in bringing an end to the conflict. Additionally, it will examine the response of the international community to the British intervention, evaluating the extent of their support and involvement.

The aftermath of the conflict presented numerous challenges for Sierra Leone's post-war reconstruction and development. The British military intervention left a lasting impact on the country's political, social, and economic landscape. This subchapter will delve into the long-term socio-economic impacts of the intervention, analyzing its effects on Sierra Leone's development trajectory. It will explore the relationship between the UK and the Sierra Leone government before, during, and after the military intervention, assessing the extent of their collaboration and cooperation.

In conclusion, the Sierra Leone conflict had far-reaching regional and global implications that continue to shape the country and its neighbors to this day. This subchapter will provide historians and enthusiasts of the British military intervention in Sierra Leone with a comprehensive analysis of the regional and global consequences of the conflict, shedding light on the complexities and dynamics that unfolded during this critical period in history.

Humanitarian and Moral Justifications for Intervention

Title: Humanitarian and Moral Justifications for Intervention

Introduction:

The 2000-2002 British Military Intervention in Sierra Leone was a pivotal moment in the country's history, marked by the devastating civil war that ravaged the nation. This subchapter aims to explore the humanitarian and moral justifications that underpinned the British intervention, shedding light on the ethical considerations and the moral imperative that drove their decision to intervene.

1. Upholding Human Rights and Preventing Atrocities:

The British intervention in Sierra Leone was driven by a commitment to protect innocent civilians and prevent further atrocities. The rebel groups, such as the Revolutionary United Front (RUF), were notorious for their brutal tactics, including mutilations and child soldier recruitment. The British saw their intervention as a means to halt these human rights abuses and restore peace to the war-torn nation.

2. Responsibility to Protect:

The concept of the Responsibility to Protect (R2P) played a crucial role in justifying the British intervention. As a member of the international community, Britain recognized its responsibility to protect the Sierra Leonean population from the horrors of the civil war. This moral obligation, endorsed by the United Nations, justified the military intervention as a means to fulfill their duty.

3. Restoring Legitimate Authority:

The British intervention aimed to restore the legitimate authority of the Sierra Leonean government, which had been undermined by rebel groups. By supporting the government, the intervention sought to uphold democratic values and strengthen the rule of law. This moral imperative was based on the belief that a stable and functioning government was essential for long-term peace and development.

4. Humanitarian Assistance and Post-War Reconstruction:

Beyond military intervention, the British forces provided crucial humanitarian assistance to the Sierra Leonean people. This included medical care, food aid, and reconstruction efforts, addressing the immediate needs of the war-affected population. The long-term goal was to support Sierra Leone's post-war reconstruction, enabling sustainable development and paving the way for a peaceful future.

Conclusion:

The humanitarian and moral justifications for the British military intervention in Sierra Leone were rooted in the principles of protecting human rights, fulfilling the responsibility to protect, restoring legitimate authority, and providing much-needed humanitarian assistance. By exploring these justifications, historians can gain a deeper understanding of the ethical considerations that guided the British intervention, its impact on Sierra Leone's post-war reconstruction, and its effectiveness in ending the civil war. Moreover, comparing this intervention with other international peacekeeping missions can provide valuable insights into the broader context of humanitarian interventions and their long-term socio-economic impacts on the development of conflict-affected nations.

Chapter 5: The Effectiveness of British Military Tactics and Strategies in Ending Sierra Leone's Civil War

Counterinsurgency Operations and Engagement with Rebel Forces

During the 2000-2002 British Military Intervention in Sierra Leone, counterinsurgency operations played a crucial role in ending the country's devastating civil war. The British Army's engagement with rebel forces was a key component of their strategy to bring peace and stability to Sierra Leone.

One of the primary objectives of the British intervention was to disrupt the activities of rebel groups such as the Revolutionary United Front (RUF). The RUF had been responsible for atrocious acts of violence, including widespread use of child soldiers, amputations, and sexual slavery. To effectively counter these insurgent forces, the British military adopted a multifaceted approach.

Firstly, the British Army focused on intelligence gathering and analysis to identify the key leaders, supply routes, and hideouts of the rebel groups. This information was used to plan targeted operations and strikes against the RUF. Special forces units were deployed to conduct precision raids, capturing or eliminating high-value targets and disrupting the rebels' command structure.

In addition to direct military action, the British Army also engaged in efforts to win the hearts and minds of the local population. They established close relationships with local communities, providing humanitarian assistance, medical care, and infrastructure development. This approach aimed to build trust among the population and undermine the support base of the rebel groups.

The British military also played a crucial role in training and mentoring the Sierra Leonean armed forces. By improving their capabilities and professionalism, the British helped to strengthen the Sierra Leonean government's ability to maintain law and order and resist future insurgencies.

The effectiveness of British military tactics and strategies in ending Sierra Leone's civil war cannot be understated. Through their counterinsurgency efforts, the British Army significantly weakened the rebel forces, leading to the eventual disarmament and demobilization of the RUF. The intervention brought a much-needed period of stability, allowing Sierra Leone to begin the challenging task of post-war reconstruction.

However, it is important to recognize that the British intervention was not without its challenges and limitations. The complexities of the conflict, the vast territory, and the dense jungle terrain made it difficult to completely eradicate all rebel elements. The RUF, although significantly weakened, continued to pose sporadic threats in the years following the intervention.

In conclusion, the British Military Intervention in Sierra Leone successfully employed counterinsurgency operations and engaged with rebel forces to end the civil war. Their tactics and strategies not only disrupted the activities of the insurgent groups but also contributed to the long-term stability and reconstruction efforts in Sierra Leone. By understanding and analyzing the effectiveness of these operations, historians can gain valuable insights into the dynamics of international peacekeeping missions and their impact on post-conflict societies. Furthermore, the lessons learned from the British intervention can inform future military interventions and efforts to promote sustainable development in conflict-affected regions like Sierra Leone.

Training and Capacity Building for Sierra Leone's Security Forces

During the 2000-2002 British Military Intervention in Sierra Leone, one of the key aspects of the operation was the training and capacity building of Sierra Leone's security forces. This subchapter explores the various initiatives undertaken by the British army to enhance the capabilities of the local security forces and the impact it had on Sierra Leone's post-war reconstruction.

The British intervention aimed not only to end the civil war but also to establish a stable and secure environment for the country's future. Recognizing the importance of a strong and capable security apparatus, the British army undertook extensive training programs for Sierra Leone's army, police, and other security forces. These programs focused on improving discipline, professionalism, and operational effectiveness.

The training initiatives included both classroom instruction and practical exercises. British military advisors worked closely with their Sierra Leonean counterparts, providing guidance and mentoring to ensure the transfer of skills and knowledge. Specialized training was also provided in areas such as counterinsurgency operations, intelligence gathering, and human rights awareness.

The impact of this training and capacity building was significant. Sierra Leone's security forces, which were previously ill-equipped and poorly trained, became more proficient and better equipped to handle security challenges. This was crucial for the country's post-war reconstruction efforts as it allowed the government to gradually assume control over security matters and reduce reliance on international forces.

Furthermore, the training programs had a positive effect on the morale and discipline of the security forces. By instilling a sense of pride and professionalism, the British intervention helped to enhance the legitimacy and credibility of Sierra Leone's security institutions in the eyes of the population.

However, challenges remained. The training and capacity-building efforts were constrained by limited resources and infrastructure. Additionally, the deep-rooted corruption within the security forces posed a significant obstacle to their long-term effectiveness. Addressing these issues required sustained international support and continued engagement with Sierra Leone's security sector.

In conclusion, the training and capacity building of Sierra Leone's security forces played a crucial role in the success of the British Military Intervention and the subsequent post-war reconstruction. By enhancing the capabilities and professionalism of the local security institutions, the intervention laid the foundation for a more stable and secure Sierra Leone. However, continued support and investment in the security sector were necessary to consolidate these gains and address the remaining challenges.

Lessons Learned and Best Practices in Peacekeeping Operations

In the subchapter titled "Lessons Learned and Best Practices in Peacekeeping Operations" from the book "Forging Peace: The 2000-2002 British Military Intervention in Sierra Leone," the focus will be on providing valuable insights and recommendations for future peacekeeping missions. This subchapter is specifically addressed to historians and individuals interested in understanding the intricacies of the 2000-2002 British Military Intervention in Sierra Leone, its impact on the country's post-war reconstruction, and the effectiveness of the British military tactics and strategies employed during the civil war.

The 2000-2002 British Military Intervention in Sierra Leone was a significant turning point in the country's history, and valuable lessons were learned from this conflict. The intervention showcased the importance of international cooperation and coordination among various stakeholders involved in peacekeeping operations. The book delves into the role played by the British Army and analyzes its strategic motives behind the intervention, highlighting the need for a well-defined and coherent political strategy in peacekeeping missions.

The effectiveness of the British military tactics and strategies employed during the intervention is thoroughly examined. The book evaluates the innovative approaches utilized by the British Army, such as the integration of humanitarian aid with military operations, and draws insights on their impact on ending the civil war. These lessons can provide valuable guidance for future peacekeeping missions, emphasizing the significance of a comprehensive approach that addresses both security and humanitarian needs.

Furthermore, the subchapter assesses the international community's response to the British intervention in Sierra Leone, shedding light on the importance of international support and collaboration in peacekeeping operations. It also extensively examines the role of local militias and rebel groups during the intervention, recognizing the complexities of dealing with non-state actors in conflict zones.

The subchapter also explores the long-term socio-economic impacts of the British military intervention on Sierra Leone's development. It analyzes the relationship between the UK and the Sierra Leone government before, during, and after the intervention, and highlights the importance of sustained engagement in post-conflict reconstruction to achieve lasting peace and development.

By comparing the British intervention in Sierra Leone with other international peacekeeping missions, this subchapter provides a broader perspective on best practices in peacekeeping operations. It encourages historians and researchers to draw insights from different experiences and adapt them to unique contexts.

In conclusion, "Lessons Learned and Best Practices in Peacekeeping Operations" offers a comprehensive analysis of the 2000-2002 British

Military Intervention in Sierra Leone, addressing the interests of historians and various niches related to the conflict. It provides valuable insights on the role of the British Army, the impact of the intervention on Sierra Leone's post-war reconstruction, and crucial lessons for future peacekeeping missions.

Chapter 6: The Humanitarian Aspect of the British Military Intervention in Sierra Leone

Protection of Civilians and Human Rights Advocacy

The British military intervention in Sierra Leone from 2000 to 2002 was not only aimed at ending the civil war but also focused on the protection of civilians and human rights advocacy. This subchapter explores the efforts made by the British Army in ensuring the safety and well-being of the Sierra Leonean population during and after the conflict.

During the intervention, the British Army recognized the importance of protecting civilians caught in the crossfire. They implemented a comprehensive strategy that included disarmament, demobilization, and reintegration programs for former combatants. These initiatives aimed to remove weapons from the hands of rebels and provide them with alternative means of livelihood, thus reducing the threat to civilians. Additionally, the British Army established safe havens and refugee camps to provide shelter and medical assistance to those displaced by the conflict.

Human rights advocacy played a crucial role in the British military intervention. Soldiers were trained in international humanitarian law and were instructed to uphold human rights standards in their operations. They closely collaborated with local and international human rights organizations to monitor and document any violations committed by warring factions. This commitment to human rights allowed the British Army to hold accountable those responsible for atrocities and contribute to the overall justice and reconciliation process in Sierra Leone.

The protection of civilians and human rights advocacy did not end with the cessation of hostilities. The British Army actively supported Sierra Leone's post-war reconstruction, focusing on strengthening the capacity of local security forces, supporting the rule of law, and promoting good governance. They assisted in the establishment of a Truth and Reconciliation Commission, which aimed to address past human rights abuses and promote healing among the Sierra Leonean population.

The impact of the British military intervention on the protection of civilians and human rights advocacy in Sierra Leone was significant. By prioritizing the safety and well-being of the population, they helped restore a sense of security and stability. Their efforts in promoting human rights and holding perpetrators accountable contributed to the country's healing process and the prevention of future conflicts.

Overall, the British military intervention in Sierra Leone demonstrated a commitment to protecting civilians and advocating for human rights. By addressing this aspect of the intervention, historians can gain a deeper understanding of the complexities and challenges faced by the British Army during this period. Furthermore, it provides insights into the long-term socio-economic impacts of the intervention on Sierra Leone's development, as a stable and secure environment is crucial for sustainable growth and progress.

Provision of Humanitarian Aid and Assistance

The provision of humanitarian aid and assistance played a crucial role in the 2000-2002 British military intervention in Sierra Leone. This subchapter will delve into the various aspects of this critical component of the operation, examining its impact on Sierra Leone's post-war reconstruction, the effectiveness of British military tactics and strategies, and the international community's response to the intervention.

The British military intervention in Sierra Leone was not solely focused on ending the civil war; it also aimed to provide much-needed humanitarian aid and assistance to the war-torn country. The British Army recognized the importance of addressing the immediate needs of the population, including food, shelter, healthcare, and protection. In collaboration with international organizations such as the United Nations and NGOs, the British forces established a comprehensive system to deliver aid to those affected by the conflict.

One of the key achievements of the British military intervention was the restoration of security, which enabled humanitarian organizations to access areas that were previously inaccessible. This facilitated the delivery of aid to remote communities, ensuring that the most vulnerable populations received the assistance they desperately needed.

The effectiveness of British military tactics and strategies in providing humanitarian aid can be seen in the successful establishment of safe zones, which offered protection to civilians and allowed aid agencies to operate freely. The British Army worked closely with local communities to identify their needs and priorities, ensuring that the aid provided was tailored to their specific circumstances.

The international community's response to the British intervention in Sierra Leone was largely positive. The coordination between the British forces and international organizations was seen as a model for future peacekeeping missions. The provision of humanitarian aid and assistance by the British Army helped to garner support and resources from international partners, contributing to the overall success of the intervention.

Furthermore, the subchapter will analyze the long-term socio-economic impacts of the British military intervention on Sierra Leone's development. It will explore how the provision of humanitarian aid and assistance during the intervention laid the foundation for post-war reconstruction and helped to address the root causes of the conflict. The subchapter will also compare the British intervention in Sierra Leone with other international peacekeeping missions, highlighting the unique challenges and successes of the operation.

Overall, the provision of humanitarian aid and assistance was a critical aspect of the 2000-2002 British military intervention in Sierra Leone. It not only helped to alleviate the immediate suffering of the population but also laid the groundwork for long-term peace and development in the country. The subchapter will provide a comprehensive analysis of this vital component of the intervention, shedding light on its impact and effectiveness.

Rehabilitation and Reintegration of Former Combatants

The rehabilitation and reintegration of former combatants played a crucial role in the success of the 2000-2002 British military intervention in Sierra Leone. As historians, it is important to understand the significance of this aspect in the overall context of the intervention and its impact on various niches, including the role of the British Army, the humanitarian aspect, and the long-term socio-economic impacts on Sierra Leone's development.

The British military intervention in Sierra Leone aimed not only to end the civil war but also to establish lasting peace and stability in the country. Recognizing the importance of rehabilitating and reintegrating former combatants into society, the intervention prioritized programs and initiatives to address their needs.

One of the key strategies employed was the establishment of disarmament, demobilization, and reintegration (DDR) programs. These programs aimed at disarming and demobilizing former combatants, providing them with psychological support, skills training, and opportunities for employment and education. By addressing the root causes of conflict and offering alternative paths to reintegrate into society, these programs played a crucial role in preventing a relapse into violence.

The effectiveness of the British military tactics and strategies in ending Sierra Leone's civil war can be attributed, in part, to the successful implementation of DDR programs. By offering incentives for combatants to lay down their arms and providing them with opportunities for a better future, the intervention was able to weaken the rebel groups and encourage defections.

Furthermore, the rehabilitation and reintegration efforts had a significant humanitarian impact on the lives of former combatants and their communities. By addressing the trauma and psychological wounds of war, these programs not only helped individuals rebuild their lives but also contributed to the healing and reconciliation of communities affected by the conflict.

In examining the long-term socio-economic impacts of the intervention, it is evident that the successful rehabilitation and reintegration of former combatants played a vital role in Sierra Leone's post-war reconstruction and development. By providing skills training and employment opportunities, the intervention empowered former combatants to become productive members of society, contributing to the country's overall economic growth and stability.

In conclusion, the rehabilitation and reintegration of former combatants was a critical aspect of the 2000-2002 British military intervention in Sierra Leone. Recognizing the importance of addressing the needs of combatants and promoting lasting peace, the intervention implemented DDR programs that played a significant role in ending the civil war and contributing to Sierra Leone's post-war reconstruction and development. This subchapter sheds light on the impact of these efforts, not only from a historical perspective but also in relation to various niches, including the role of the British Army, the humanitarian aspect, and the long-term socio-economic impacts on Sierra Leone's development.

Chapter 7: Assessment of the International Community's Response to the British Intervention in Sierra Leone

Role of the United Nations and International Organizations

The role of the United Nations (UN) and international organizations in the 2000-2002 British military intervention in Sierra Leone was crucial in achieving peace and stability in the war-torn country. This subchapter aims to analyze their involvement and the impact it had on the conflict and subsequent post-war reconstruction.

The UN played a pivotal role in facilitating the peace process in Sierra Leone. The deployment of the United Nations Mission in Sierra Leone (UNAMSIL) in 1999 marked a significant turning point. UNAMSIL's mandate was to disarm rebel groups, monitor the ceasefire agreement, and support the restoration of state authority. The UN's involvement provided a framework for the British military intervention and ensured international legitimacy for the operation.

International organizations such as the Economic Community of West African States (ECOWAS) and the African Union (AU) also played important roles. ECOWAS, through its military arm ECOWAS Monitoring Group (ECOMOG), had been involved in the conflict since its outbreak in 1991. ECOMOG's efforts to maintain peace and protect civilians laid the groundwork for the British intervention. The AU supported the peace process by providing diplomatic and logistical assistance.

The coordination between the UN, ECOWAS, and the AU was instrumental in achieving the primary objective of the intervention – ending the civil war. The combined efforts of these organizations helped secure a ceasefire agreement, disarm rebel groups, and pave the way for the reestablishment of state authority. Their involvement also ensured the protection of civilians and the provision of humanitarian aid to those affected by the conflict.

Furthermore, the UN and international organizations played a crucial role in Sierra Leone's post-war reconstruction. They provided assistance in rebuilding infrastructure, promoting good governance, and supporting economic development. The UN's Peacebuilding Commission, established in 2005, specifically focused on long-term reconstruction efforts in Sierra Leone.

In conclusion, the United Nations and international organizations played a vital role in the 2000-2002 British military intervention in Sierra Leone. Their involvement provided legitimacy, coordination, and support for the intervention, leading to the end of the civil war and laying the groundwork for post-war reconstruction. Their efforts not only helped bring peace and stability to Sierra Leone but also contributed to the long-term socio-economic development of the country.

Support and Contributions from Other Countries and Donors

The 2000-2002 British Military Intervention in Sierra Leone received significant support and contributions from various countries and donors, which played a crucial role in its success and the subsequent reconstruction of Sierra Leone. This subchapter examines the international community's response to the intervention and the long-term socio-economic impacts it had on Sierra Leone's development.

From the outset, the British intervention garnered widespread international support. Countries such as the United States, Canada, Nigeria, and Ghana provided crucial logistical and financial assistance. The United States, for instance, contributed military equipment and provided intelligence support to the British forces. Canada, on the other hand, offered humanitarian aid and played a key role in training Sierra Leone's security forces.

Furthermore, international organizations such as the United Nations, the European Union, and the African Union, among others, also made significant contributions. The United Nations Peacekeeping Mission in Sierra Leone (UNAMSIL) worked closely with the British forces, providing logistical support and helping to stabilize the situation on the ground. The European Union provided financial aid for the reconstruction efforts, while the African Union deployed peacekeepers to ensure the sustainability of peace and security in Sierra Leone.

Donor countries and organizations also played a critical role in supporting Sierra Leone's post-war reconstruction. Financial aid and technical assistance were provided to help rebuild the country's infrastructure, strengthen its institutions, and promote socio-economic development. The International Monetary Fund and the World Bank, for instance, provided financial support and debt relief to facilitate Sierra Leone's recovery and development.

The contributions from other countries and donors were instrumental in the success of the British military intervention in Sierra Leone. They not only provided the necessary resources and assistance but also demonstrated international solidarity and commitment to ending the civil war and supporting Sierra Leone's transition to peace.

Furthermore, the long-term socio-economic impacts of the British military intervention were also influenced by the support and contributions from other countries and donors. The assistance provided facilitated the rebuilding of infrastructure, revitalized the economy, and improved access to education and healthcare. It also helped strengthen democratic institutions and promote good governance, laying the foundation for sustainable development in Sierra Leone.

In conclusion, the support and contributions from other countries and donors were vital in the success of the British military intervention in Sierra Leone. The international community's response played a significant role in stabilizing the situation, supporting post-war reconstruction, and fostering long-term socio-economic development. The collaborative efforts demonstrated the importance of international cooperation in resolving conflicts and promoting peace and development in war-torn countries like Sierra Leone.

Cooperation and Coordination among International Actors

In the subchapter titled "Cooperation and Coordination among International Actors," this section delves into the intricate web of collaboration and coordination between various international actors during the 2000-2002 British Military Intervention in Sierra Leone. Historians, particularly those interested in the 2000-2002 British Military Intervention to End Sierra Leone's Civil War, will gain valuable insights into the role of international players and their contributions to the resolution of the conflict.

The British military intervention in Sierra Leone was not a standalone effort but rather a result of international cooperation. This subchapter explores the alliances forged among different countries, organizations, and institutions to address the complex challenges faced during the intervention. It highlights the critical role played by the United Nations, African Union, Economic Community of West African States (ECOWAS), and the Commonwealth, among others.

The effectiveness of the intervention is analyzed through an examination of the strategies and tactics employed by the British military. Historians interested in the role of the British Army in Sierra Leone's Civil War will find an in-depth assessment of the military's approach, including its successes and shortcomings. The humanitarian aspect of the intervention is also explored, shedding light on the efforts made to protect civilians, provide humanitarian aid, and restore order and stability.

Moreover, this subchapter provides an assessment of the international community's response to the British intervention. It analyzes the support, cooperation, and contributions of other countries, organizations, and non-governmental entities in the intervention. The examination of the role of local militias and rebel groups during the British intervention in Sierra Leone offers a comprehensive understanding of the complex dynamics at play during the conflict.

The subchapter also delves into the UK's relationship with the Sierra Leone government before, during, and after the military intervention. It explores the dynamics of this relationship, including the challenges faced and the cooperation established to ensure a successful outcome.

Furthermore, this section offers a comparative analysis of the British intervention in Sierra Leone with other international peacekeeping missions. Historians interested in the broader context of peacekeeping efforts will find valuable insights into the similarities, differences, and lessons learned from these missions.

Lastly, this subchapter addresses the long-term socio-economic impacts of the British military intervention on Sierra Leone's development. It examines how the intervention influenced the country's post-war reconstruction, economic growth, and social progress. Historians studying the impact of international interventions on a nation's development will find this analysis particularly relevant.

Overall, this subchapter provides a comprehensive exploration of the cooperation and coordination among international actors during the 2000-2002 British Military Intervention in Sierra Leone. It offers historians a nuanced understanding of the intervention's complexities, its impact on Sierra Leone's post-war reconstruction, and its broader implications for international peacekeeping efforts.

Chapter 8: Examination of the Role of Local Militias and Rebel Groups during the British Intervention in Sierra Leone

Analysis of Local Militias and Their Influence on the Conflict

In the subchapter "Analysis of Local Militias and Their Influence on the Conflict," we delve into the intricate dynamics of the Sierra Leone civil war and the role played by local militias. This analysis is crucial for historians seeking a comprehensive understanding of the 2000-2002 British military intervention in Sierra Leone and its impact on the conflict.

The local militias in Sierra Leone were disparate groups with varying objectives, often aligned with different rebel factions. These militias, such as the Kamajors and the Civil Defense Forces, emerged as important actors in the conflict, wielding considerable influence over local communities and exerting control over territories. Their activities ranged from providing security and protection to engaging in acts of violence and perpetrating human rights abuses.

Understanding the motives and actions of these local militias is essential in assessing the effectiveness of the British military intervention. The British forces had to navigate a complex landscape, engaging with various armed groups while simultaneously trying to restore stability and protect the civilian population. The analysis of the local militias provides insights into the challenges faced by the British troops and the strategies they employed to achieve their objectives.

Furthermore, the influence of local militias on post-war reconstruction cannot be overlooked. As the conflict subsided, the British intervention aimed to support the disarmament, demobilization, and reintegration process. However, the presence and power of local militias posed significant obstacles, as they often resisted efforts to disarm and persisted in their control over certain regions. This analysis sheds light on the difficulties faced by the British forces in disbanding these militias and the implications for Sierra Leone's long-term peace and development.

By examining the role of local militias, historians gain a nuanced understanding of the complexities of the Sierra Leone civil war and the British military intervention. This analysis provides valuable insights into the broader themes of the book, including the political and strategic motives behind the intervention, the effectiveness of British military tactics, and the long-term socio-economic impacts on Sierra Leone's development.

In conclusion, the analysis of local militias and their influence on the conflict offers a crucial perspective on the British military intervention in Sierra Leone. By exploring their motives, actions, and impact on post-war reconstruction, historians can gain a comprehensive understanding of this pivotal period in Sierra Leone's history and its implications for international peacekeeping efforts.

Engagement with Rebel Groups and Efforts to Facilitate Peace

In the subchapter "Engagement with Rebel Groups and Efforts to Facilitate Peace," we delve into the intricate web of relationships between the British military and rebel groups during the 2000-2002 intervention in Sierra Leone. This chapter aims to provide historians and enthusiasts of the British military intervention with a comprehensive understanding of the strategies employed to end Sierra Leone's civil war and foster long-lasting peace.

The British military intervention marked a turning point in Sierra Leone's history, as it sought to put an end to a decade-long conflict that had ravaged the nation. One of the key challenges faced by the British forces was the need to engage with various rebel groups operating within Sierra Leone, such as the Revolutionary United Front (RUF) and the Armed Forces Revolutionary Council (AFRC). Understanding the dynamics of these rebel groups was crucial in formulating effective tactics and strategies to bring about peace.

This subchapter explores the different approaches taken by the British military to engage with rebel groups. It analyzes the negotiations, disarmament processes, and the integration of former combatants into society. By examining these efforts, historians can gain insights into the complexities of peacebuilding in a post-conflict environment.

Additionally, this chapter evaluates the impact of these engagement strategies on Sierra Leone's post-war reconstruction. The success of the British military intervention in facilitating a relatively stable and peaceful Sierra Leone is analyzed, with a particular focus on the long-term socio-economic impacts and the development of the nation.

Furthermore, this subchapter examines the political and strategic motives behind the British intervention in Sierra Leone. By analyzing the decision-making process, historians can gain a deeper understanding of the UK's geopolitical interests in the region and its commitment to humanitarian intervention.

In conclusion, "Engagement with Rebel Groups and Efforts to Facilitate Peace" offers historians a comprehensive analysis of the British military intervention in Sierra Leone. By examining the strategies employed to engage with rebel groups and foster peace, as well as the long-term impacts on Sierra Leone's development, this subchapter sheds light on the complexities of international peacekeeping missions and the challenges of post-conflict reconstruction.

Disarmament and Demobilization of Local Militias

In the subchapter titled "Disarmament and Demobilization of Local Militias," we delve into the crucial process undertaken by the British military during the 2000-2002 intervention in Sierra Leone. This topic holds immense significance for historians, particularly those interested in the British military intervention to end Sierra Leone's civil war and its subsequent impact on the nation's post-war reconstruction.

The disarmament and demobilization of local militias formed a pivotal part of the British strategy in achieving lasting peace in Sierra Leone. This subchapter aims to provide a comprehensive analysis of this process and its various dimensions.

We begin by exploring the reasons behind the disarmament and demobilization efforts, focusing on the need to neutralize the threat posed by local militias and rebel groups. By disarming these factions, the British military aimed to create a conducive environment for the successful implementation of peace agreements and the subsequent reconstruction of Sierra Leone.

Next, we delve into the specific tactics and strategies employed by the British military during the disarmament and demobilization process. This includes an examination of the challenges faced, such as the voluntary surrender of weapons, the identification and verification of combatants, and the provision of reintegration support. We analyze the effectiveness of these strategies in disarming and demobilizing local militias, ultimately contributing to the end of Sierra Leone's civil war.

Furthermore, we explore the humanitarian aspect of the disarmament and demobilization efforts, highlighting the British military's commitment to safeguarding the well-being of former combatants. We discuss the provision of humanitarian assistance, such as medical care, psychological support, and skills training, to aid in the reintegration process and promote long-term stability.

Additionally, this subchapter assesses the international community's response to the British intervention in Sierra Leone, particularly in terms of supporting the disarmament and demobilization process. We analyze the role of various organizations and countries in providing resources and expertise to facilitate the successful implementation of this critical aspect of the peacebuilding process.

Finally, we examine the long-term socio-economic impacts of the disarmament and demobilization process on Sierra Leone's development. Through a comparative analysis with other international peacekeeping missions, we evaluate the unique aspects and challenges faced by the British intervention in Sierra Leone, shedding light on the lessons learned and best practices for future interventions.

Overall, the subchapter on "Disarmament and Demobilization of Local Militias" offers historians a comprehensive and nuanced understanding of the British military's efforts to end Sierra Leone's civil war and contribute to the nation's post-war reconstruction. It sheds light on the specific challenges, strategies, and impacts associated with the disarmament and demobilization process, providing valuable insights for scholars interested in both the historical and humanitarian aspects of conflict resolution and peacebuilding.

Chapter 9: The UK's Relationship with the Sierra Leone Government before, during, and after the Military Intervention

Historical Ties and Diplomatic Relations

The subchapter titled "Historical Ties and Diplomatic Relations" delves into the longstanding relationship between the United Kingdom and Sierra Leone, providing crucial context for understanding the 2000-2002 British Military Intervention in Sierra Leone. This chapter addresses the interests and motivations behind the British intervention, evaluates the effectiveness of their strategies, and examines the impact of the intervention on Sierra Leone's post-war reconstruction.

To comprehend the reasons behind the British intervention, it is essential to explore the historical ties and diplomatic relations between the two nations. Sierra Leone, a former British colony, had a complex and intertwined relationship with the UK, dating back to the 18th century. The chapter begins by tracing the historical ties, highlighting the factors that shaped the UK's interest in Sierra Leone and its subsequent involvement in the country's affairs.

Drawing upon historical records and diplomatic correspondence, this subchapter provides a comprehensive analysis of the political and strategic motives that led to the British intervention. It explores the UK's concerns over regional stability, the threat posed by rebel groups, and the potential for Sierra Leone's conflict to spill over into neighboring countries. Additionally, it evaluates the humanitarian aspect of the intervention, emphasizing the UK's commitment to protecting civilians and fostering long-term peace.

The effectiveness of British military tactics and strategies in ending Sierra Leone's civil war is a critical aspect of this subchapter. Through a detailed examination of military operations, the chapter assesses the success of the British intervention in restoring stability and disarming rebel groups. It considers the challenges faced by the British Army and the innovative approaches they employed to overcome them.

Furthermore, this subchapter discusses the international community's response to the British intervention in Sierra Leone. It evaluates the level of support and cooperation received from other countries and international organizations, shedding light on the significance of this mission within the broader context of international peacekeeping efforts.

Finally, this chapter examines the long-term socio-economic impacts of the British military intervention on Sierra Leone's development. It analyzes the role of local militias and rebel groups during the intervention, considering their influence on the outcome and the subsequent challenges faced during the post-war reconstruction process.

Overall, "Historical Ties and Diplomatic Relations" provides a comprehensive analysis of the 2000-2002 British Military Intervention in Sierra Leone. Addressed to historians and readers interested in the intricacies of the intervention, this subchapter offers valuable insights into the motivations, strategies, and impacts of this critical period in Sierra Leone's history.

Collaboration and Cooperation in Conflict Resolution

In the subchapter "Collaboration and Cooperation in Conflict Resolution" of the book "Forging Peace: The 2000-2002 British Military Intervention in Sierra Leone," we delve into the crucial role of collaboration and cooperation in ending Sierra Leone's civil war. This section aims to provide historians and those interested in the British military intervention with a comprehensive understanding of the various actors involved in the conflict resolution process.

The 2000-2002 British Military Intervention to End Sierra Leone's Civil War witnessed a remarkable display of collaboration and cooperation among different stakeholders. The British Army, alongside the Sierra Leone government, local militias, rebel groups, and the international community, worked together to bring about peace and stability in the war-torn nation.

Analyzing the political and strategic motives behind the British intervention, we shed light on how collaboration with the Sierra Leone government was pivotal in achieving the desired outcomes. The book explores the complexities of this relationship before, during, and after the military intervention, providing insights into the challenges and successes faced by both parties.

Furthermore, this subchapter delves into the effectiveness of British military tactics and strategies in ending Sierra Leone's civil war. By examining their collaborative approach with local militias and rebel groups, historians can gain a deep understanding of how these alliances contributed to the conflict resolution process. The book also critically assesses the international community's response to the British intervention, highlighting the importance of international cooperation in achieving sustainable peace.

The humanitarian aspect of the British military intervention is another crucial aspect explored in this subchapter. The book delves into the efforts made by the British Army to provide humanitarian aid and support to the war-affected population. It assesses the extent to which collaboration with local communities and international humanitarian organizations contributed to the success of the intervention.

Additionally, this subchapter offers a comparative analysis of the British intervention in Sierra Leone with other international peacekeeping missions. By examining the similarities and differences, historians can gain valuable insights into the unique challenges and strategies employed in Sierra Leone.

Lastly, this section explores the long-term socio-economic impacts of the British military intervention on Sierra Leone's development. By assessing the collaborative efforts made in post-war reconstruction and development projects, historians can evaluate the lasting benefits and challenges faced by the nation.

Overall, the subchapter "Collaboration and Cooperation in Conflict Resolution" provides a comprehensive analysis of the various collaborative efforts made during the British military intervention in Sierra Leone. It offers valuable insights for historians and individuals interested in understanding the complexities and outcomes of this intervention, while also shedding light on the broader themes of conflict resolution and peacekeeping.

Post-Intervention Engagement and Support for Sierra Leone's Government

In the aftermath of the British military intervention in Sierra Leone, the focus shifted from ending the civil war to supporting the country's government and facilitating post-war reconstruction. This subchapter delves into the various aspects of post-intervention engagement and support provided by the British to Sierra Leone's government, shedding light on the long-term impacts of the intervention.

The British military intervention in Sierra Leone, spanning from 2000 to 2002, successfully brought an end to the country's devastating civil war. However, the task of rebuilding a war-torn nation and ensuring sustainable peace was equally challenging. The post-intervention period witnessed concerted efforts from the British to assist Sierra Leone's government in consolidating its power and kick-starting the process of reconstruction.

One of the key aspects of post-intervention engagement was the establishment of a comprehensive training program for the Sierra Leonean armed forces. The British military played a significant role in training and equipping Sierra Leone's military and police forces, enabling them to effectively maintain law and order in the country. The training program focused not only on enhancing combat skills but also on promoting professionalism, respect for human rights, and adherence to the rule of law.

Furthermore, the British government provided substantial financial assistance to Sierra Leone's government for post-war reconstruction efforts. This assistance encompassed various sectors, such as infrastructure development, healthcare, education, and economic revitalization. The aim was to create an enabling environment for sustainable development and to address the root causes of the conflict.

In addition to financial aid, the British government also extended diplomatic and political support to Sierra Leone's government. This support was crucial in helping the government navigate the complex post-war political landscape, fostering stability, and building trust among different factions. The British diplomats worked closely with their Sierra Leonean counterparts, offering guidance and expertise to promote good governance, democracy, and respect for human rights.

The post-intervention engagement and support of Sierra Leone's government by the British played a significant role in the country's post-war reconstruction and development. The interventions not only helped to restore a sense of normalcy but also laid the foundation for long-term socio-economic progress. The training and equipping of Sierra Leone's armed forces contributed to the establishment of a secure environment, while financial aid and diplomatic support bolstered the government's capacity to deliver essential services and foster stability.

Overall, the British military intervention in Sierra Leone was not just a short-term military operation but a comprehensive endeavor to support the country's government and facilitate long-term peace and development. The chapter explores the effectiveness of these efforts, analyzes their impact on Sierra Leone's reconstruction, and assesses the enduring socio-economic consequences of the intervention. Historians and those interested in the British role in Sierra Leone's civil war and its aftermath will gain valuable insights into the complexities of post-intervention engagement and support.

Chapter 10: Comparison of the British Intervention in Sierra Leone with Other International Peacekeeping Missions

Similarities and Differences in Mandates and Strategies

The 2000-2002 British Military Intervention in Sierra Leone was a pivotal moment in the history of the country's civil war. Understanding the similarities and differences in mandates and strategies employed during this intervention is crucial for historians studying various aspects related to this event and its aftermath.

The mandate of the British military intervention was primarily focused on restoring peace and stability to Sierra Leone, ending the brutal civil war that had plagued the country for over a decade. Similarly, other international peacekeeping missions often share this objective of establishing a peaceful environment in conflict-ridden regions.

However, what sets the British intervention in Sierra Leone apart from other missions is the unique strategy employed by the British Army. Unlike traditional peacekeeping missions, the British intervention had a more robust and aggressive approach. The British forces actively engaged with rebel groups and local militias, aiming to dismantle their operations and bring an end to the conflict. This approach differed from the more passive and defensive strategies adopted by many other peacekeeping missions.

The effectiveness of the British military tactics and strategies in ending Sierra Leone's civil war cannot be understated. The intervention successfully disarmed and demobilized rebel groups, restoring a sense of security and stability to the country. This outcome is attributed to the British Army's comprehensive approach, which combined military operations with humanitarian efforts, such as providing aid and support to the local population.

The humanitarian aspect of the British military intervention in Sierra Leone was another distinguishing feature. While the primary objective was to end the conflict, the British forces also played a crucial role in providing humanitarian assistance to the war-affected population. This approach demonstrated the commitment of the British Army to not only bring peace but also to contribute to the long-term reconstruction and development of Sierra Leone.

Comparing the British intervention in Sierra Leone with other international peacekeeping missions reveals both similarities and differences. While the mandate of restoring peace is shared among these missions, the strategies and approaches employed may vary significantly. The British intervention's unique blend of military operations and humanitarian efforts sets it apart from many other missions.

The long-term socio-economic impacts of the British military intervention on Sierra Leone's development are also worth examining. The intervention not only ended the civil war but also created a foundation for post-war reconstruction and development. Understanding these impacts is crucial for historians studying the role of the British intervention in shaping Sierra Leone's trajectory after the conflict.

In conclusion, the similarities and differences in mandates and strategies employed during the 2000-2002 British Military Intervention in Sierra Leone provide valuable insights for historians studying various aspects related to this event and its aftermath. The unique blend of military operations and humanitarian efforts, along with the long-term socio-economic impacts, distinguishes this intervention from other international peacekeeping missions and highlights its significance in Sierra Leone's history.

Lessons Learned and Transferable Practices

The subchapter titled "Lessons Learned and Transferable Practices" in the book "Forging Peace: The 2000-2002 British Military Intervention in Sierra Leone" offers a valuable analysis of the British military intervention and its impact on Sierra Leone's civil war, post-war reconstruction, and long-term development. Historians interested in various aspects of this intervention will find this subchapter particularly insightful, as it examines the key lessons learned and transferable practices that can be applied to similar international peacekeeping missions in the future.

One of the crucial lessons highlighted in this subchapter is the importance of a comprehensive and integrated approach in conflict resolution. The British military intervention demonstrated the significance of combining military force with diplomatic negotiations, humanitarian aid, and post-war reconstruction efforts. By addressing the root causes of the conflict and engaging with local communities, the British Army successfully contributed to ending the civil war and promoting stability in Sierra Leone.

Additionally, the subchapter delves into the effectiveness of British military tactics and strategies employed during the intervention. It assesses the innovative methods used, such as the deployment of small teams to train and support Sierra Leonean forces, as well as the successful disarmament and demobilization programs implemented. These practices can serve as valuable examples for future peacekeeping missions seeking to achieve sustainable peace and security in post-conflict societies.

Furthermore, the subchapter explores the humanitarian aspect of the British military intervention. It emphasizes the importance of providing humanitarian assistance alongside military operations, ensuring the well-being of affected populations and facilitating the delivery of essential services. This holistic approach not only helped to address immediate humanitarian needs but also contributed to building trust and cooperation between the military and local communities.

The subchapter also examines the role of the international community in responding to the British intervention in Sierra Leone. It critically evaluates the support and contributions of various actors, highlighting the importance of international cooperation and coordination in achieving common goals. Moreover, it discusses the UK's relationship with the Sierra Leone government, analyzing the dynamics before, during, and after the military intervention.

Finally, the subchapter explores the long-term socio-economic impacts of the British military intervention on Sierra Leone's development. It assesses the efforts made in rebuilding infrastructure, strengthening governance institutions, and promoting economic growth. By examining these impacts, historians can gain valuable insights into the challenges and successes of post-conflict reconstruction and development.

In conclusion, the subchapter "Lessons Learned and Transferable Practices" in "Forging Peace: The 2000-2002 British Military Intervention in Sierra Leone" provides a comprehensive analysis of the British intervention and its implications for Sierra Leone's civil war, post-war reconstruction, and long-term development. Historians interested in various aspects of this intervention will find this subchapter an essential resource, as it offers valuable lessons and transferable practices for future peacekeeping missions and sheds light on the complex dynamics between the military, local communities, and the international community.

Contribution to the Evolution of Peacekeeping Norms and Practices

The 2000-2002 British Military Intervention in Sierra Leone played a significant role in shaping the evolution of peacekeeping norms and practices. This subchapter explores the contributions made by the British intervention to the field of peacekeeping and its impact on Sierra Leone's post-war reconstruction.

The British military intervention in Sierra Leone marked a turning point in the international community's approach to peacekeeping. The intervention demonstrated the effectiveness of a robust and proactive approach to conflict resolution, emphasizing the protection of civilians and the restoration of law and order. This approach challenged traditional peacekeeping practices that focused primarily on monitoring ceasefires and separating warring factions.

The British Army's role in Sierra Leone's civil war was instrumental in bringing an end to the violence and restoring stability. Through a combination of military tactics, intelligence gathering, and engagement with local communities, the British forces successfully disarmed rebel groups and militias, dismantled illicit diamond networks, and supported the Sierra Leone government in regaining control over the country. These efforts not only ended the immediate conflict but also laid the groundwork for long-term peace and development.

Furthermore, the humanitarian aspect of the British military intervention cannot be overlooked. British forces provided crucial support in addressing the humanitarian crisis caused by the civil war, including the protection of civilians, the provision of food and medical aid, and the establishment of safe zones for internally displaced persons. These actions set a precedent for the integration of humanitarian assistance into peacekeeping operations, emphasizing the importance of addressing the root causes of conflict and ensuring the welfare of affected populations.

The international community's response to the British intervention in Sierra Leone was overwhelmingly positive. The intervention was widely seen as a model for future peacekeeping missions, with its emphasis on comprehensive strategies, cooperation with local actors, and the protection of civilian populations. Lessons learned from the British intervention influenced subsequent peacekeeping efforts in other conflict zones, contributing to the evolution of peacekeeping norms and practices.

In conclusion, the 2000-2002 British Military Intervention in Sierra Leone made significant contributions to the evolution of peacekeeping norms and practices. The robust and proactive approach demonstrated by the British forces challenged traditional peacekeeping methods and emphasized the importance of protecting civilians and restoring law and order. The intervention's impact on Sierra Leone's post-war reconstruction and its influence on subsequent peacekeeping missions further solidified its place in the history of international peacekeeping efforts.

Chapter 11: Long-Term Socio-Economic Impacts of the British Military Intervention on Sierra Leone's Development

Economic Recovery and Reconstruction Efforts

The economic recovery and reconstruction efforts following the 2000-2002 British military intervention in Sierra Leone played a crucial role in stabilizing the war-torn country and laying the foundation for long-term development. This subchapter will delve into the various initiatives undertaken to rebuild Sierra Leone's economy and the impact of these efforts.

Immediately after the conflict, the British government recognized the urgent need to address the economic devastation caused by the civil war. They implemented a comprehensive plan that focused on revitalizing key sectors, including agriculture, mining, and infrastructure. By investing in these areas, the British aimed to create employment opportunities, boost economic growth, and improve living conditions for the population.

One of the significant achievements was the restoration of the diamond industry, which had been a major driver of the conflict. The British military intervention helped establish a transparent diamond certification process, ensuring that the revenue generated from diamond exports would benefit the country rather than fuel further conflict. This move not only contributed to economic growth but also helped restore international confidence in Sierra Leone's diamond trade.

Furthermore, the British government provided financial support for infrastructure projects, such as road construction and the rehabilitation of basic utilities like electricity and water supply. These initiatives aimed to improve connectivity and provide essential services to the population, creating an environment conducive to economic growth.

In addition to these efforts, the British military intervention also focused on capacity-building and training programs for local businesses and entrepreneurs. By equipping the local population with the necessary skills and knowledge, the intervention aimed to empower individuals, reduce unemployment, and promote sustainable economic development.

The economic recovery and reconstruction efforts in Sierra Leone after the British military intervention were not without challenges. The country faced significant obstacles, including limited resources, institutional weaknesses, and corruption. However, despite these hurdles, the intervention helped lay the groundwork for long-term socio-economic development.

In conclusion, the economic recovery and reconstruction efforts following the 2000-2002 British military intervention in Sierra Leone played a vital role in stabilizing the war-torn country. Through initiatives targeting key sectors and capacity-building programs, the intervention aimed to revitalize the economy, create employment opportunities, and improve living conditions. While challenges persisted, the intervention provided a solid foundation for long-term development in Sierra Leone.

Socio-Economic Challenges and Obstacles

The socio-economic challenges and obstacles faced by Sierra Leone in the aftermath of the civil war were immense. The 2000-2002 British military intervention played a crucial role in bringing an end to the war, but the task of rebuilding and reconstructing the nation was far from over. This subchapter explores the various socio-economic challenges and obstacles that hindered Sierra Leone's post-war reconstruction.

One of the main challenges was the widespread poverty and unemployment that plagued the country. The civil war had devastated the economy, leaving many Sierra Leoneans without jobs or means of livelihood. The British military intervention aimed to restore stability and create an environment conducive to economic growth. However, the process of rebuilding the economy was slow and hampered by limited resources and lack of infrastructure. This hindered the government's efforts to provide employment opportunities and alleviate poverty.

Another obstacle was the issue of land ownership and displacement. During the war, many people were forced to flee their homes and lands, resulting in a massive displacement of the population. The return and resettlement of these individuals posed a significant challenge. The British military intervention worked towards facilitating the return of displaced people and supporting the government in implementing land reforms. However, the process was complex and often marred by conflicts over land ownership, making it difficult to achieve sustainable solutions.

Furthermore, the post-war period saw an increase in crime and lawlessness, which had a detrimental effect on the socio-economic development of Sierra Leone. The British military intervention focused on disarming and demobilizing rebel groups and militias. However, the reintegration of former combatants into society proved challenging as many struggled to find employment and adjust to civilian life. This led to a rise in criminal activities and hindered efforts towards stability and development.

In addition, the lack of access to basic services such as healthcare and education posed significant challenges to Sierra Leone's development. The civil war had destroyed many schools and healthcare facilities, leaving communities without vital services. The British military intervention aimed to support the government in rebuilding these institutions and providing access to essential services. However, the process was slow, and the quality of services remained inadequate in many areas.

Overall, while the British military intervention played a crucial role in ending Sierra Leone's civil war, the challenges and obstacles faced in the post-war period were immense. The socio-economic development of the country was hindered by poverty, unemployment, land disputes, crime, and lack of access to basic services. The efforts of the international community, including the UK, were instrumental in addressing these challenges, but long-term sustainable solutions were required to overcome these obstacles and forge a path towards peace and development.

Sustainable Development and Future Prospects for Sierra Leone

Sierra Leone, a country scarred by a brutal civil war, has made significant strides towards sustainable development since the British military intervention that ended the conflict in 2002. This subchapter delves into the post-war reconstruction efforts in Sierra Leone, analyzing the long-term socio-economic impacts of the British military intervention and exploring the future prospects for the country.

The British military intervention in Sierra Leone played a crucial role in bringing an end to the civil war that ravaged the country for over a decade. The intervention not only restored peace but also laid the foundation for sustainable development. The British army's tactics and strategies were effective in dismantling rebel groups and disarming militias, paving the way for a more stable and secure environment.

One of the key aspects of the British military intervention was its humanitarian focus. The international community responded positively to the intervention, providing aid and support for Sierra Leone's post-war reconstruction. This assistance was instrumental in addressing the immediate needs of the population, such as healthcare, education, and infrastructure development.

The relationship between the UK and the Sierra Leone government before, during, and after the military intervention was crucial in ensuring the success of the reconstruction efforts. The UK's commitment to supporting Sierra Leone's long-term development remained steadfast, and this partnership played a significant role in fostering political stability and economic growth.

Comparisons with other international peacekeeping missions highlight the unique challenges faced by the British intervention in Sierra Leone. The country's history of diamond-fueled conflict and the involvement of local militias and rebel groups presented complex dynamics that required a tailored approach. The British military's ability to adapt and work alongside local actors was key to achieving sustainable peace.

Looking towards the future, Sierra Leone's prospects for sustainable development are promising. The long-term socio-economic impacts of the British military intervention have been positive, with increased investment, improved infrastructure, and a growing economy. However, challenges such as poverty, corruption, and political instability still persist, requiring continued international support and cooperation.

In conclusion, the British military intervention in Sierra Leone had a significant impact on the country's post-war reconstruction and development. The intervention not only brought an end to the civil war but also laid the foundation for sustainable peace and economic growth. Sierra Leone's future prospects for sustainable development are promising, but continued support and collaboration from the international community are vital to ensure long-term success.